THE REPUTABLE REP

SUCCESS IN SALES AND LIFE

SIG SCHMALHOFER

THE REPUTABLE REP

SUCCESS IN SALES AND LIFE

PART 1

INTRODUCTION

THE SECRET CAREER

The biggest challenge in the manufacturer's rep business is explaining to people outside of our world what we actually do. Why do we pack the trunks of nice cars with reams of brochures and odd looking displays and samples that would never make it through airline screening?

When loading a truck with a barbeque, coolers, tables, and all the trimmings, my neighbors believe my company is in the catering business. I invite them to the wholesaler grand opening we're sponsoring and even provide an address. Amazingly, they never attend! If my mom asks what I have planned for the week, she scratches her head when I tell her I'll be in Las Vegas on Monday to meet with a builder about a new project and in San Diego on Tuesday for a distributor open house. She looks at me puzzled. "I thought I raised you to use common sense!" I just smile. After all, this is a labor of love! When I proceed to tell her that on Wednesday I'm picking up a regional manager from LAX and heading to a dinner meeting with a contractor in Santa Maria, she's mystified. She has no idea that the regional is a great guy that I love hanging with and that the customer is one of my best friends! I smile.

After explaining that on Thursday I'll be taking the factory man to Lancaster for a job walk with a plumber having problems with our product, it's a given; she concludes I've lost my mind. I reply, "It will be fine. I keep a pair of Levis, tennis shoes, and a hard hat in my car!"

After my final comment about hosting a Friday 6 AM coffee and donut training meeting with a large repair plumber in Culver City, followed by a trip back to LAX, my mom exhaustedly apologizes for asking about my plans and calls me a 'no hoper'. Noting a concern, I reassure her, "Don't worry about me. I'm well aware of the damage that donuts can do to my body, so I offer the donuts, but I don't eat any of them." I can't blame her for asking what on earth I'm talking about. I simply reply that I don't even indulge in the donut that has a special place in my heart: the apple fritter!

My golf buddies get indignant when I explain to them that I can't play on Sunday because our agency is hosting a hundred customers at a Chargers' tailgate. They shake their head and tell me I live in a world of my own.

I reply, "Well it's not completely a world of my own. Amazingly, other people have stumbled upon this secret career that isn't a job, but rather an adventure!"

My law enforcement and teacher friends wonder why, without a guaranteed pension at the end of the rainbow, I spend days futilely attempting to satisfy the opposing needs of customers and factories. They wonder why I have chosen to act as a translator who mediates disputes between factories and customers, each speaking a different language. When explaining that planning a future with a 30-day contract is not as bad as it might sound, family members wonder how a human being conceived from the same gene pool could have possibly chosen this secret business that defies any concept of logic. Again, I smile!

> "Reps work on straight commission and survive day to day with no guarantees. Nonetheless, because of their confidence, they stay the course. That's real risk taking!"
>
> — **Joe Cicora, National Sales Manager, Red White Valve**

Have you ever driven past a construction site and wondered what brands of products are being used, what contractor is installing them, and where they were purchased?

If you aren't a tradesman, rep, or distributor living in the secret world of industrial wholesale distribution, you merely treat construction zones as a nuisance. Not so for those of us existing in our secret world where people that work with the tools, like plumbing contractors, are worshipped.

As for products that are sold inside big retail stores, the marketing of those products is clearly different. Our discussion of the secret career of being a manufacturer's rep involves sales, marketing, and distribution of products sold in the wholesale channel. This is where the plumbers, electricians, and heating and air contractors of the world, buy their materials. This business segment is secret because if you're not a contractor, a distributor, or a participant in my secret world, you probably have no idea who sells these products, nor do you care. You are in the vast majority of people who have no idea what a manufacturer's rep is and what they actually do. Simply stated, the business of the manufacturer's rep is to contract with manufacturers in a common industry to act as their exclusive sales and marketing arm in a defined territory.

The business is sometimes referred to as a sales agency or a rep firm. These companies typically employ anywhere from 1 to 50 adventure seekers who have miraculously stumbled into this secret business. Smaller rep companies might have a handful of lines they represent. Larger firms could have two dozen or more. When going to market, a factory seeking to sell their brand of products in the wholesale arena has two choices:

*Hire and train their own sales force to call on distributors and create demand for these distributors by working the secondary market. The manufacturers bear the cost of salaries, cars, expenses, and benefits. This is an expensive proposition that requires significant up front costs. Ramping-up new people in a new industry is slow and costly with no guaranties that there will be a return on the investment. Nonetheless, many successful manufacturers use this strategy.

OR

*Hire a manufacturer's rep operating in their industry within a target area. If a factory manufactures water heaters, they'll hire a plumbing rep. If a factory manufactures refrigerators, they'll hire an appliance rep.

Agencies are paid a percentage of sales.

This marketing strategy is attractive to manufacturers because they are not fronting the cost of an expensive sales force that has little local knowledge, industry savvy, or personal relationships in the market. Manufacturer's reps are entrenched in markets selling other products in the same industry to familiar buyers. They leverage their expertise in an industry.

They use personal relationships with buying influences to launch or revitalize sales of product lines into a market.

Reps eagerly enter into these factory relationships with short term contracts and few guarantees. They are eternal optimists that believe their smarts, contacts, and diligence will create sales commissions.

Here's a note from my friend Steve Shipley, a former

Reputable Rep:

> "I covered all of Southern California and Las Vegas, rumbling down the road in my Ford van; loaded with drain equipment for demonstrations and counter days. One morning, I was working Las Vegas; generating lots of interest at Familian's counter. Evidently the branch manager was impressed. After watching the excitement from his office he told me that he was also responsible for Utah. He offered to put my product into his Utah branches if I would cover them. I didn't hesitate. 'Of course I will! Thank you very much!' That eternal optimism created additional sales but also added 1,200 additional miles of driving to the enormous market I already covered. The result? After many road trips of torturing my body, I left the rep business and took a job with a wholesaler!!"
>
> **— Steve Shipley, Hirsch Pipe and Supply**

Reps are always in search of manufacturers introducing a new product which will change their secret world. They are like stock investors searching for a penny stock with the potential to be a blue chipper.

So, you may ask, what kind of people seek the secret world of manufacturer's reps? This, of all the questions I have been asked, is the easiest to answer: "Knuckleheads like me!"

I supported my way through college working in a plumbing shop. Because unloading trucks, digging ditches, and getting my hands grimy from threading pipe did not seem to be my calling, I vowed to never look back once I became an educator. After all, teaching is a wonderful career that nurtures the minds and attitudes of our next generations.

But after teaching for 3 years I did what I said I never would do. I left the world of teachers' unions, job security, and pension guarantees to enter the business world, accepting an offer from Moen, a wonderful company that is a leader in the faucet business. While working at Moen, I was not a manufacturer's rep; I was a factory salesman with a good salary, nice bonus program, a company car plus expenses and a great package of benefits that included a retirement pension.

I loved working for Moen. I was certain that nothing would top my career there. After all, I was increasing business astronomically, winning sales awards, and earning huge bonuses!

But, as I worked my territory, I discovered the secret world of manufacturer's reps. A world that guarantees none of the things that Moen generously supplied, but fulfilled the American Dream of becoming an entrepreneur whose success was dictated by hard work, creativity, and an unabashed determination to be responsible for one's own destiny. I learned that the secret world of manufacturer's reps was exhilarating and offered the potential to be very rewarding!

Smart sales agencies around me had unlimited earning opportunities and the independence to get things done their way.

So, I made another risky move. Even though I was supporting a young family, I accepted an offer to be a salesman for Sales Support, an upstart manufacturer's rep business that had just been appointed the rep firm for Delta Faucet Company, Moen's major competitor. This experience made me hunger for my own agency. But in my life of detours, I chose an alternate route that put me into the wholesale plumbing business; an episode that in the recession of the late 80s and early 90s brought me to my knees and tested every fiber of resolve I could muster up! Broke, and in desperate need of a career rebound, in 1993 I considered starting my own manufacturer's rep businesses.

I'm not sure why, but through thick and thin my wife, Beverly, has stuck with me; through the most wonderful of good times and the most depressing bad times imaginable.

But, a manufacture's rep is not a rep unless he has a line to sell. That's the story within the story. Never underestimate the power of good fortune. And yes, I got lucky. I found one of those penny stocks that through tireless work became a super blue chipper. The factory that I took on, more by desperation than design, was Bradford White, a start-up water heater manufacturer that industry pundits said would fail. Because I had friends who would be calling the shots, I was not deterred. Carmen Catania, Bradford White's newly appointed western regional manager is still my mentor and lifelong friend. Bob Carnevale, the inspirational leader who was then the president of the fledgling company, is now Chairman of the Board and my hero! I moved forward with Signature Sales riding Bradford White, a horse many picked to finish last. I optimistically picked the newcomer to win the race. I moved forward and entered the secret world of manufacturer's reps.

However, the decision was not an easy one. I had many friends at Moen. My guardian angel, Roger Garrison, had rolled out the carpet for me to return.

I was overwhelmed, but I had a gut feeling that returning to Moen would be a step backwards. I wondered if I should seek a management position for the new Bradford White. Noting my reluctance to plunge into the rep business with the upstart company, Bob Carnevale lectured me, "You are going to be my rep! You are going to be a damn good one. And mark my words: you will earn lots of money with this line!"

So it began! My agency started with a desk in my garage and then inched its way into the dining room. But time behind that desk was reserved for late nights, Saturdays, and Sundays. To be successful, I traveled the highways of Southern California and Southern Nevada in my tired Caravan...all day...every day...with one hand on the steering wheel and the other on my mobile phone. To become viable and ultimately successful, I knew I needed to execute a well thought out business plan which called for me to convince target distributors and contractors that Signature Sales and Bradford White had formed a team they needed to be on. In later years, I asked an industry legend who owned a very successful distribution business, why he decided to become a Bradford White customer. His response, "Sig, from the time I first met you, I determined that it would be smarter for me to sell with you than against you!"

In my career in this secret business, I have received no greater compliment.

Fast forward to 2016. Today, Bradford White is an industry leader. The company I founded, Signature Sales, now employs 42 people, and we are honored to represent some of the most successful factories in the plumbing industry.

In 2014, our agency was honored as the first ever Rep of the Year by a respected industry publication, *Reeve's Journal*. Twenty-three years after Signature was founded, Bradford White still represents the foundation of Signature's thriving business. A new team of owners are leading the Signature Sales charge: my son Nick Schmalhofer and daughter Katie Hubach plus my 'quasi-adopted' sons, Jeremy Crane and Arron Sanders. My middle child, Lisa, is making a career out of my first career, teaching.

I'm delighted to say her teaching makes the world a better

place to live in every single day. My wife of 44 years still thrives as Signature's controller. My friend Ron Bradford, the partner I took on in 1994, is still calling on specifying engineers and making a difference.

And me? Because it's such a joy, I'm still active in the agency, but also loving my second career as a writer. I find great joy in sharing my experiences in a life filled with overcoming challenges and succeeding in a business that has been very rewarding.

In 1996, three years after starting Signature Sales, I was diagnosed with Limb Girdle Muscular Dystrophy.

Over the years, friends and colleagues have noticed I struggle a bit getting from point A to point B. Years ago, observing my unique stride, a contractor friend nicknamed me Ratchet-Ass, a name that has, in some circles…stuck! Until recently, I've been reluctant to make my ailment public because I was determined to succeed in spite of my handicap and without spilling the beans about my secret physical challenge.

Yes, my family knew and my closest friends knew, but for the most part, no one knew.

Why did I not broadcast this news? I just couldn't bear the thought of people feeling sorry for me. As Larry Schafer says in my book, *Jelly Beans 2, 'Trails'*, "Pity for me, is pitiful". Since I now walk with a cane, find stairs impossible to climb, and struggle to lift my golf bag, many people are well aware of Sig's muscular dystrophy story.

If you weren't aware, I'm happy that I did a good job of keeping my secret. But now, here it is: written proof that I am among *Jerry's Kids*.

This is my third book. The first two are fictional by definition but based on my real life experiences. *Jelly Beans in*

Life and *Jelly Beans in Life 2*, will soon be followed by *Jelly Beans in Life 3*.

After introducing my book *Jelly Beans in Life*, my friend Bob Carnevale told me…

> "What you really should do is write a book about how to be a good rep!"
>
> — **Bob Carnevale, Chairman of the Board,**
> **Bradford White Corporation**

Bob, once more, I'm following your guidance. I hope you're not disappointed!

I've been fortunate to have many wonderful mentors who have taught me the art of being a good rep. Wise customer friends have taught me many lessons; especially explaining what good reps do and what bad reps neglect.

And some stuff, believe it or not, I just figured out myself. In this, my first non-fiction book, I share the secrets for being successful in the secret business of being a manufacturer's rep.

The sales principles discussed are relevant to anyone that makes a living as a salesman on the road. The strategies contained in this unique sales tutorial are drawn from my career in the plumbing industry, but can be applied universally.

"It is a rare thing in this day and age to have employees that stay in one position for extended periods of time. The regional sales manager role has about 80% of the people (for most manufacturers) falling in two buckets.

Bucket 1: High performers who continue to move up the ladder within the company or find better positions within the industry. Either way, they promote out of the role.

Bucket 2: Those who hang in the role for 18-60 months before they move on or get fired. Are there exceptions? Of course!

The manufacturer's representative is the constant gardener of market relationships and provides the stability manufacturers need during times of employee transition. Manufacturers talk endlessly about driving the secondary market. Given that time is money, especially for the rep, it is prudent for the manufacturer to sell their reps on a return on their time investment. Then, listen to the feedback."

— **Kendrick Reaves, Reliance Worldwide**

THE SECRET BUSINESS

If being a manufacture's rep is a secret career, then plumbing is the secret business.

When the word 'plumbing' comes to mind, most people think of the scenario above. They think about the guy who drags a drain snake to a home to unplug a toilet.

It's seen as a nasty job that, unfortunately, somebody has to do. So, when I tell people that I work in the plumbing industry, the reaction is predictable. They think I'm the guy with the drain snake. When I tell them that I'm in the plumbing industry but I'm not a plumber, they conclude I must sell toilets. Needless to say, neither unclogging toilets nor selling them is glamorous.

> "When I worked for Kohler, my four-year old daughter asked me what my job was. I smiled and told her that I sold toilets. With the honesty only a child possesses she replied, 'No way Daddy! You're a liar!'"
>
> **— Chris Semerau, Director of West US Sales, Reliance Worldwide**

I find it interesting that millions of people are filing for unemployment while plumbing manufacturers, distributors, and contractors ask me every single day if I know anyone looking for a job. It's absolutely mind-boggling that the plumbing industry offers some of the most exciting career opportunities available anywhere in any industry, but job applicants are scarce.

Even more puzzling is that no one can dispute the basic premise that plumbing is no nickel and dime industry! Sales of plumbing fixtures alone (like the one shown in the picture) are 12 billion dollars a year.

To support engineering, manufacturing, distribution, marketing, and sales on fixtures alone, an army of people collect very nice paychecks, and more people are needed!

Manufacturers like Moen Faucet, Delta Faucet, Kohler, American Standard, InSinkErator, A.O. Smith, Bradford White, and Rheem, to name a few, are names many consumers recognize. But to the average American, these brands do not translate to jobs. Why? I've rattled my brain to solve the mystery! The only plausible answer is that plumbing is not glamorous. Apple? They're glamorous. And so are scores of other techy companies. I have a son-in-law who is a product manager for Toyota. A second son-in-law is an engineer for Direct TV, now a subsidiary of AT&T. When I observe the fathers of my grandchildren in a social setting, talking about their jobs and their sexy products, it becomes crystal clear that careers in automobiles and televisions are cool. Everybody is interested in new models, new gadgets, and new toys that will be available for TVs and cars! Toilets? Water heaters? Faucets? Not so much! Boilers? Forget about it! How about plastic pipe or fittings? Regulators? I just don't think so! Garbage disposers? Not a chance? Whirlpools? Maybe…provided free samples are available!

Now a story about trading in a career in a cool, sexy business for wholesale plumbing.

> "I was honored to participate in an amazing factory trip to China with folks from Gerber, Sig and Nick Schmalhofer, and Bill Glockner, the President and CEO of my employer, Hirsch Pipe and Supply. At dinner, I was prompted to describe the career path that led me to the plumbing industry. I explained that in my earlier years, I was in the recording business for a company that is now a giant in the syndicated radio business, 'Westwood One'. After a sip of wine, I bemoaned my fate. 'If I was still in that business, no telling where I'd be!' Bill Glockner, the man who signs my paychecks, took note and calmly said, 'Hmm, business class flights, Mission Hills Resort in Shenzhen, China, 5-star dining! Good question! I wonder where you'd be?'
>
> Never failing to take advantage of an opportunity, at a future meeting Bill presented me with Westwood One business cards, and for the group, Westwood One scratch pads."
>
> **— Bob Berumen, Hirsch Pipe and Supply**

One of the reasons I've written this book is to attract people to our wonderful industry, even though it's not glamorous or cool. My dream is for the 'Reputable Rep' to find its way into the hands of young people looking for a rewarding career. The dynamic opportunities will overwhelm the lack of glamour and coolness.

"The plumbing industry isn't for everybody. But neither is a life on Wall Street or the world of courtrooms and litigation. When I was recruited by companies looking for young, ambitious people, I was intrigued by Ferguson because they offered opportunity with the caveat that I would need to earn it. That meant learning the business from the bottom, toiling in tasks like manhandling 50,000 pounds of copper. Eighty hours would be the norm for trainees. To me, it sounded like a challenge. Since a deeply rooted work ethic was part of my make-up, I was intrigued. So, I chose a career with Ferguson. The opportunity was 2,000 miles away. I loaded my pick-up with all my worldly possessions and left Virginia for a new life and challenge in Fort Lauderdale, Florida. My career started with a competition between a roommate trainee and me. If my shift called for me to be at work at 7, I arrived at 6:30; triggering the appropriate response from my roommate: He showed up at 6:00 AM! You guessed it! I then arrived at 5:30. And so it went! But, I loved the challenge! I remember a sarcastic plumber needling me to fill his order before butterflies emerged from their cocoons. I ran to the warehouse. Yes, I ran! Like Tom Sawyer with the challenge of painting a fence, I made a game out of it. With teamwork from my friends in the warehouse, we delivered that order in record time, and well before butterflies emerged. When I was challenged to work nights digging ditches for a good customer, I accepted! No, it wasn't glamorous, but it was what I signed up for. In one word, it was a competition. A competition I made a commitment to win! The result was the career with Ferguson that I wanted! I've never looked back! Ever!"

— **Ron Kern, Ferguson Enterprises**

If you, or someone you know, are young, ambitious, and up for a challenge, interview with a plumbing manufacturer, distributor, contractor, or manufacturer's rep. You'll be pleasantly surprised at what you'll find! Our secret world, if it's discovered, is believed to be stodgy. Not so! Like most anything in life, it's what is done with an opportunity that predicates exhilaration or boredom.

Louie Armstrong of Ferguson Enterprises combines the powerful tools of 'off the chart' energy, humor, and imagination to make our industry great!

"I walked into the buyer's office of a huge contractor only to find my competitor, Paul Morelli, already there. The buyer was excited! She said it was the perfect storm! She was ready to order a truckload of Western Pottery round front toilets. She gave us each a piece of paper and asked us to quote her our best price. The low bidder would win the order. The bids were returned. The buyer reviewed them. She looked Paul in the eye and told him that the order was going to me. Paul, who was rarely under-bid, was furious. 'How is that possible?' She calmly told him that my bid simply stated '2% less than Paul!'"

— **Louie Armstrong, Ferguson Enterprises**

PART 2

SALES FOUNDATIONS

COLD CALLS

Prospecting is typically a cold call, but a cold call with a purpose. Possessing the fearless willingness to walk into a sales call where 'you know no one' and 'no one knows you' is critical. In the story below, a wholesaler sales rep investigates a potential new market. The result was a career changer!

"I came out of college at the age of 22 and followed my father's path into the wholesale plumbing industry. After four months working in the warehouse and at the sales counter, I had wreaked enough havoc on a forklift and complained just enough that I was given an opportunity in outside sales. I was to call on 50 service and repair plumbers in West L.A. My customer list contained a great group of plumbers who had been in business for decades. These businesses had operated generation to generation doing plumbing service work primarily for apartment complexes. Although I had built a great relationship with the customers and grew my business with them, the milk run became monotonous; three faucet stems here, a garbage disposer there, etc. I wanted more. One day on my milk run, I had an epiphany! As I drove past the Beverly Hilton Hotel, I challenged myself to make them a customer. Surely they required plumbing supplies for their repairs! It was logical that a fancy hotel, charging top dollar for a night's stay, would not let a faucet leak! So, I did some prospecting! I made a cold call at the Beverly Hilton. It was not a good one. It was horrible!

I was young, naïve, and parked my car out front at the valet. At the reception desk, I asked, 'Who fixes your plumbing when it goes bad?' Since it was obvious that I had no clue what I was doing, I was given a business card for the Director of Engineering, who saw sales people by appointment only.

My first attempt to sell plumbing to a hotel was a failure! Plus, it cost me $20 for the privilege of parking my car for a few minutes. Nevertheless, I was determined to figure it out.

I sought advice from my dad, who was a pretty good salesman. Without hesitation, he told me I had gone to the wrong side of the hotel. I needed to return to the Beverly Hilton and park in the back, where I would find salesmen cars like the Ford Taurus and Chevy Celebrity. He told me that sales people that came through the front door needed appointments; not so for the clever sales people that came through the back door.

Finally, he lectured me not to look lost, but to act like I knew what the hell I was doing! I thanked him for the advice. Right before I hung up, he emphasized, 'Don't forget to bring donuts! You've got to bring donuts!'

I had nothing to lose, so I followed every bit of his advice. I returned to the Beverly Hilton the next morning, making my way to the back of the property. As advertised, Taurus and Celebrity cars were parked with business cards in their windows. A memorable 'Coors Brewing Company' card caught my attention. I put my company business card in the window of my car just like the other sales guys. I then walked through the back door of the hotel with confidence, just as I had been instructed! I walked down the hall and entered a door that said 'Hotel Engineer', acting 'like I knew what I was doing'! Now I was face to face with a man that looked to be in his nineties.

He asked, 'Who the hell are you?' I extended the open box of donuts towards him and with a smile I said, 'I'm Dean. I'm here from the supply house to sell you plumbing parts.' After rifling through the box with the dirtiest hands I've ever seen, he said, 'I'm Billy. I'm the lead plumber! Follow me!'

Billy got on his 'walkie talkie' and mumbled something I couldn't understand. Five minutes later, 10 hotel engineers entered the stock room, cigarettes in mouths, coffee in hands, eagerly selecting donuts. That was the beginning of a beautiful success story.

Like clockwork, every Tuesday I was in that stock room writing orders for plumbing parts, lots of plumbing parts. I was ecstatic! I thought nothing could be better than this! I had reached the pinnacle of my career!

Eight months later, still armed with an order pad and a box of donuts, I was summoned to Merv Griffin Enterprises, the owner of the Beverly Hilton.

I was introduced to the hotel GM, a designer, an architect, a project manager, and the general contractor for the hotel's upcoming renovation. It was a short meeting. The general manager boldly introduced me to the group, 'This is our guy! He takes care of our hotel plumbing supplies, and we want to use him for the renovation!' After exchanging cards, my head started spinning. I really couldn't believe it. Really? Was all of this possible?

A few days later, the general contractor called me and forwarded the entire material list for the renovation. The plumbing supplies on the job represented more sales dollars than I would realize in an entire year for all my accounts!

I had never been involved in anything like this. It was on the job training, but still, somehow I supplied the job without a single hiccup. The hotel was thrilled with my service.

As the job was wrapping up, the general contractor handed me a set of blueprints for a job in New Orleans that they were awarded. He bluntly declared, 'Here's the next job I want you to supply us!'

I was overwhelmed! I flashed back to how everything started; having a hunch that triggered a cold call; taking my dad's advice to make the sales call through the back door; acting like I knew what I was doing, when in fact, I had no clue.; and of course, remembering to bring the icebreaker: a box of donuts. From there, things snowballed, and then snowballed some more. As they say, the rest is history."

— Dean Armstrong, Ferguson Enterprises

My friend Dean turned a cold call into a career at Ferguson that has taken him far beyond the job of an enterprising salesman. Today, he is Ferguson's National Manager of Renovation and Hospitality!

Cold calls are definitely a tool that can move the ball forward. Fact-finding, like identifying decision makers, can be helpful in developing strategies. Asking smart questions to discover information that will be useful for future planned appointments is valuable for achieving goals.

Cold calls can be a Hail Mary that actually connects for a touchdown! You'll find more true life stories in this book that prove it!

GETTING IT!

The Reputable Rep must have curiosity. He needs to ask himself questions like, "I wonder if the local water district could benefit from my water-saving products?" He needs to be able to connect the dots that separate opportunity and success.

The Reputable Rep has a fire in his belly that fuels success and makes it contagious!

> "It's easy to become successful in this business. Just be there 24/7 and do what you say you are going to do!"
>
> **— Steve Grosslight, Ferguson Enterprises**

Reputable Reps will go to extraordinary lengths to do what it takes to get the job done. That's called 'Getting it'!

> "My Kansas City rep sold a Highland Tank oil water separator system to a chemical manufacturing plant and had to do a follow-up meeting. In order to be allowed in the facility for the meeting, he had to wear the proper breathing equipment. To accomplish that, he had to shave his beard and mustache. Now that's dedication!"
>
> **— Tom Schoendorf, Highland Tank**

LISTEN AND LEARN

The number one cause of 'Death by Rep' is talking too much. Chatterboxes are annoying in business. A relatively new phenomenon is, 'Death by PowerPoint'. All of us have experienced the pain that a presenter can inflict when they read every word on every over-whelming slide shown. PowerPoints can be effective if the art of conversing is not neglected. They need to be short and lively.

If presentations using PowerPoints are the core of your sales strategy, do a self-evaluation of your skills as a speaker. It may be smart to attend a class on public speaking. These seminars are well worth the investment of time and money.

All too often, canned pitches and formal presentations can be the death of a sale. In the end, smart questions and intense listening win the day.

A scripted presentation does not take into account the critical ingredient of a business proposition: the needs of the customer.

> "A Reputable Rep must be a good listener. He must identify the needs of the customer before trying to sell anything!"
>
> **— Bob Berumen, Hirsch Pipe and Supply**

STORY TIME: ENCYCLOPEDIA BILL

Several years ago we represented a line of commodity products with a catalogue that was overwhelming.

The factory sales manager made a joint sales call with us that became the best example of worst practices I've ever witnessed. This was the first call with the national sales manager I'll call *Encyclopedia Bill*.

Our meeting was with the purchasing manager of a large multi-branch distributor. After a few pleasantries, Encyclopedia Bill opened his intimidating catalog. Then, the race was on.

At a frantic pace, he reviewed every product on every page, leaving no opportunity for anyone in the meeting to squeeze in even a peep. Eye contact was nonexistent. Gauging buyer interest was no concern. Finally, we could endure no more. Encyclopedia Bill was interrupted. He looked up with a smile, eyes wide open. His response was even more astonishing.

"Thank you for allowing me to get all the way to page 29. That's the furthest I've ever gotten in my presentation!"

Did we win over this customer? Of course not! That was an extreme example of 'death by rep' or factory sales manager. In the business of selling, addressing the needs of the customer wins the day. Asking clever questions identifies the needs. Listening to the customer leads to intelligent conversation.

Once the Reputable Rep identifies a win-win proposition, by listening, good things have a chance to occur.

STORY TIME: SPA PLUMBING

The year was 1979. I know many of my readers were not yet born in 1979, but like classical music, sales stories are timeless. I'm a Moen salesman who stumbles on a way to sell $12 bar sinks for $17.

Jim Birmingham, a grumpy Canadian who was far more comfortable in a tavern than an office, was my teacher. I'll never forget the sign hanging prominently in his office:

> "PLEASURE! EVERYONE GIVES IT!
> SOME BY ENTERING A ROOM, SOME BY LEAVING IT!"

Most visitors were intimidated. I thought of it as a win-win. Jim would be happy with me either way. I walked into Spa Plumbing, a dominant and respected union plumbing shop, at 6 AM.

It was summer in the low desert. To accommodate large flocks of snowbirds, a country club building boom was in full swing. Plumbers started their days early to beat the heat. Jim was the purchasing agent. I showed him my sample: an Excalibur 15x15 bar sink that had a basket strainer drawn into the stainless steel sink body. The look was seamless and clean, but that's not what got me the business.

Jim studied my prized contraption. He turned the sink upside down and spun the locknut onto the built-in shank. I stood quietly as the wheels in his head spun like a merry-go-round. He aggressively slammed buttons on his calculator. He looked up at me and slammed the buttons again. "What's my price," he barked. I handed him a quote from one of his suppliers, Hajoca. He mumbled words with his Canadian accent that I could barely hear or understand.

He sat quietly again, then responded, "I've been paying $12 for Polar sinks. Your sink will cost me $5 more."

I fumbled for words to justify my price but he had completed his analysis and was ready to get me out of his office so he could move on to the next task on his list. Jim took a brief moment to explain his decision. "Including their benefit package, my union plumbers cost me $75. Most of my guys are old and methodical, but we can live with them being slow because we rarely have call backs. This sink will cut installation time in half!"

I interjected, "You're also getting a better looking sink with clean lines. Plus, you save a connection and a potential leak!"

Jim didn't smile. He never smiled!

"Tell Sean at Hajoca I'll need 200 sinks a month for the next 6 months. It's your responsibility to make sure I don't run out! If I do run out, I'll hunt you down! It won't be pretty!"

I'd like to take credit for the clever sales angle employed at Spa Plumbing but really, the best thing I did was to shut up and listen. There's some wisdom there as well. The net result was that I sold more bar sinks than the rest of the territories in the United States combined. After all, bar sinks around the country were rarities, but they were standard equipment in the desert. It felt great to be the Excalibur bar sink king!

NEED-SATISFACTION SELLING

There are countless books written and seminars available on the topic of need-satisfaction selling.

I attended a seminar that referred to this skill as finding the customer's pain and magically healing it.

Simply stated, it's all about listening.

By listening to the customer the Reputable Rep discovers the customer's needs. By asking smart questions, the Reputable Rep discovers how he can help them. Utilizing the tools he has, he then provides the customer with potential solutions.

TRAINING

A fundamental truth is that no man going into battle on his own can defeat an army. By training associates at the counter, in the showroom, and on sales desks, Reputable Reps can impact a market in a huge way. Training technicians in plumbing shops or in the rep's in-house training facility is essential. It's a huge difference maker!

Sadly, most distributor sales people that reps rely on to sell their products have little to no sales training. Teaching salesmanship and ultimately how to sell your product can be both personally and economically satisfying.

> "A Reputable Rep must model the sales behavior that they want the distributor's sales staff to emulate."
>
> **— Bill Glockner, President/CEO Hirsch Pipe and Supply**

Over the years, I've taught sales classes and rewarded participants with certificates to acknowledge graduation from a product knowledge class. Incredibly, I still see these certificates posted above desks in the market. Some of them are now 10-15 years old. I always made it a point to have prizes for smart answers and tests that encouraged a competitive spirit without embarrassment.

Allowing the students to check their own test against the correct answers insured a positive experience.

Trade organizations offer classes to apprentices.

It's smart business to train the next generation of contractors on the installation and service of the products you represent.

ASKING FOR THE ORDER

There are countless ways to make a deal, close a sale, or get an order. The one common denominator requires the strategy sales reps are reluctant to use: asking for the order. Asking for an order should never be abrupt. The conversation should just flow in that direction. This is the final step of the process. But, let's rewind to the beginning. I've always believed that the objective of a sales call should be to 'SELL' without the customer having the feeling they were being SOLD. I don't think anyone likes to be SOLD anything. Many of us have walked off of car dealership lots because we felt we were being SOLD!

The ideal sales call occurs with conversations that feel like they are between friends sitting on a balcony, enjoying a cigar or sharing a drink. How can a rep create a similar experience?

Relax the mood! How about the typical meeting that is in an office? A clever sales rep can relax a mood. Holding a cup of coffee in one hand and a briefcase in the other is a terrific way to soften the mood of a meeting. Getting the customer to go out and grab a bite to eat is ideal. Meetings over lunch have a relaxing pace that mixes personal relationship building with business. If a rep is doing his job, getting a customer out to breakfast or lunch should be a piece of cake.

I view most of my customers as friends. I care about them and their families. I know a little bit about their kids, their hobbies, their likes, and of course, their dislikes. Why? Because we are friends doing business.

When that's the case, a productive meeting can be in a restaurant, a patio, or a stark office.

Some customers don't take the time to go out for lunch. That's fine. On the way to their office, call them and tell them you're bringing lunch. Ask them what they are in the mood for. In time, you won't need to make that call. You'll know what their favorite foods are. It might be lox and bagels. It might be a ham and cheese sandwich from a local deli. When a rep has this kind of meeting, asking for the order is a naturally occurring outcome. It's unforced and easy!

The next story illustrates how a Reputable Rep, enjoying a meal with a customer, can ask for help in an easy way. Note that all of this takes place in a conversation...not in a presentation.

STORY TIME: THE RIO HOTEL

In the mid-eighties, I made the change from being a Moen factory man to working for an upstart manufacturer's rep agency that was just awarded the Delta Faucet line. Part of my territory was Las Vegas, which I had worked hard to make a 'Moen Town'. I had a feeling that converting business from Moen to Delta in this part of my territory would be a challenge, but I underestimated the difficulty. I had caught a few small fish in the river, but it was full of large fish business opportunities. The fact of the matter was that I had not cracked a game changer.

I made a call on Kelly's Pipe and Supply, a key distributor who was entrenched in the new hotel construction business. The owner was a staunch Moen distributor and my friend, George Shoen.

As was our ritual, we went out for breakfast. George was the rare customer who insisted on picking up the check...every time! After he asked me how it was going for me, I told him I was a bit frustrated. It was quite a job undoing what I had done! He shook his head empathetically. I asked him for help, I asked him if he had any lead on a new hotel that I could follow up on. Did he have a mechanical engineer I wasn't already calling on that was working up specs on a new project? George was always in the know. He knew about every project that was coming up and who the decision makers were. He always had inside knowledge on secret projects that no one knew about.

I prided myself in knowing my territory. I was pretty good at monitoring the job information I received from Dodge reports, but George always had the key to the lock that opened the door to secret business.

He was a kind man with a huge heart. Plus, George

possessed an amazing knowledge of the market.

He compassionately told me that he knew how hard I worked and that I deserved a better fate. He would see to it that Delta was put onto the first phase of a huge job ready to break. He went on to say it would be a marquee project that would one day be famous.

As you can imagine, I was ecstatic! I peppered him with questions, "Who was the engineer; who was the room designer; who had the inside track to be the general contractor; who would win the contract to do the plumbing?"

George smiled. "I know you're a bird dog that would call on all those people and make a compelling argument with each of them, but this job is a gift to you for being my friend. You need not call on anyone."

I was puzzled.

George had a twinkle in his eye. "I'm the decision maker and Kelly's is supplying all the plumbing!" I still didn't get it. George finally let the cat out of the bag. "Sig, the hotel will be called The Rio. It will be built on Flamingo Road! I'm part owner!"

The construction of the Rio continued phase after phase well beyond my tenure as the Delta rep. I still smile and think about George Shoen every time I drive by the Rio Hotel!

SMART QUESTIONS

This discussion needs to start with the inverse. What are the dumb questions that reps ask that have nothing to do with anything? Asking dumb question after dumb question about the big game played the night before is 'death by rep'. Making a topic out of the weather is 'death by rep'.

Spreading rumors about a competitor or another rep is 'death by rep'.

What are some smart questions? Let's pretend Larry is in a meeting with a customer we'll call Curly. After a few, very short pleasantries, Larry gets down to business.

Larry: It's a crazy business climate out there. What are you seeing out there on water heaters?

Curly: My competitors are idiots. They're dipping deep into their backside for every damn order!

Larry: 40s and 50's I suppose.

Curly: Of course!

Larry: Who's enemy number one?

Curly: Super Cheap Supply!

Larry: Maybe you should diversify a little bit. Perhaps put your effort into something more profitable.

Curly: Like what?

Larry: Commercial water heaters. Margins are a lot better on commercials!

Curly: We don't sell many commercials. Every once in a while we'll get an order for one by accident. That's about it.

Larry: If you bought them right you could price them right, sell more, and still make a nice profit!

Curly: Okay, you're sucking me in. How do I do that?

Larry: By becoming a commercial stocking distributor. I could get you a great deal if you ordered 24 at a time.

Curly: It will take me forever to sell 24!

Larry: What if I helped you? I'm tight with some plumbers that would like to buy my commercials, but since you don't have them in stock at the right price, they buy them from 'Plumb Crazy'. That costs us both a sale. As you know, 'Plumb Crazy' doesn't stock my product.

Curly: Twenty-four commercials? Man, that's a big investment! Can I really make money on them?

Larry: Don't forget that when you sell them heaters, you've

got their attention. You'll have a good shot at getting some of their other business.

Curly: Good point!

Larry: I'm pretty sure you'll love the margins on commercials; plus, the new business will be a big plus!

Curly: Makes sense!

Larry: Let me do some leg work. I'll find out what the key contractors are paying for 199s and 250s. Once I'm armed with that info, I'll call the factory and then get back to you.

Curly: Thanks a million, Larry!

Farfetched you say? Probably a little bit. But not that far from a real life conversation a rep could be and should be having with a customer.

In that scenario, Larry put himself in the powerful position of being the customer's consultant. In our world, it doesn't get any better than that!

THE DECISION MAKER

The above strategy can be successful provided the rep is calling on the decision maker. In my career, I have seen countless sales people waste enormous time and energy naively knocking on the wrong door; spinning their wheels, wasting time calling on someone that has zero influence on the decision, and praying that the decision maker somewhere downstream will get the message.

The decision maker might be above or below the prospect incorrectly being targeted. I've seen factory people wine and dine the top dog, who ultimately defers to his team or 'Go-To-Guy'.

Likewise, a purchasing agent can be targeted by a rep when in fact their purchasing power is limited to buying products approved by the real decision maker.

The Reputable Rep knows who to target. He has the knowledge of the local players in the market and knows who the ultimate decision maker is.

THE EXTRA CALL

The best athletes in the world, no doubt, are blessed with exceptional bodies, balance, and coordination. However, that alone, does not allow them to achieve maximum success. The desire to be the best fuels their need to go the extra mile. High achievers are always on the lookout for something that gives them an edge. The Reputable Rep has the same mindset. They out-plan, out-research, and out-work the competition.

A good way to accomplish excellence is to push yourself further than you thought you would go, even after you determine your day is done. At the end of a long day, make one extra call, which could very well become the difference-maker.

STORY TIME: ARROYO GRANDE

It was 1994. I was working the central coast, the region of my territory that had no Bradford White distributors. After getting another 'no', this time from a national distributor in Paso Robles, I asked a contractor at the counter to please name the distributors he did business with. All the names he gave me had already given me a 'no', except one: Streator Pipe.

The contractor commented that Streator was a small wholesaler located on an alley in the tiny town of Arroyo Grande.

The time was 4:40. I was determined to make that one extra call! If I hustled, I could be in Arroyo Grande by 5:30.

I arrived to find a chain link gate rolled shut with the padlock hanging, but not locked. Parked in front of the entrance was a white truck. I took a chance. I rolled the gate open and walked into the pipe yard only to find, in the far end, a busy man with a clipboard busily counting his inventory.

He looked up, obviously surprised to see an intruder. "What are you doing here? We're closed!"

I handed him a card and replied, "My name is Sig, and I sell Bradford White water heaters."

The young man was a bit annoyed but introduced himself, "Mike Streator. I've never heard of that brand. I buy American Appliance heaters!" Since a re-distributor in the Central Coast was well-known for selling American water heaters to smaller distributors, I asked the obvious question, "Who do you buy them from?"

"Big Time Wholesale."

"Aren't they your biggest competitor?" Mike answered emphatically, "Yes!"

"Isn't it hard to compete against your supplier?"

The answer to the question was no different than the chain link fence that Mike had left open, allowing us to meet. "I have no choice. American won't sell me heaters direct!"

A simple close to the deal followed. "I will!"

Mike smiled. I gave him a two-minute pitch about Bradford White's philosophy.

My soon-to-be longtime friend shook his head and smiled again. "Sounds like I need to be a Bradford White distributor. Come by in the morning and we'll work out a program and pricing. I get here at 6:30!"

"See you at 6:30; I'll spring for the donuts!"

Mike Streator and I have been friends for over twenty years. We love retelling the story about two desperate guys who helped each other get started in business. The only thing Mike likes better than laughing about that story, is taking my money on the golf course!

PART 3

SALES PREPARATION

APPOINTMENTS

In this, the age of instant communication, appointments with customers and clients is critical. Surprise hit and run sales calls are rarely effective. The exceptions, of course, are drive-by stops delivering samples, literature, etc.

However, as discussed in the previous chapter, cold calls on a hunch, mining for business, should be in every Reputable Rep's playbook.

PLANNING

I grew up in the business being taught, 'Plan your Work and Work your Plan'. It's still relevant. Early in my career, after attending a seminar, I began using the Franklin Planner system. It's still available and continues to be a great tool.

The key take-away is to have a system that works well for daily activities, long term strategic planning, and foolproof follow-up. The particular system chosen is less important than the commitment to using it religiously.

When making a sales call, have specific goals for the outcome. Prepare mentally by rehearsing in your mind the exchange of ideas you are anticipating. Jason Day, the number one golfer in the world today, visualizes every shot before he swings.

Readiness is critical. I remember making a key call on a homebuilder from New Jersey who opened operations in my territory. I was an eager salesman working with Bill O'Neil, the national builder sales manager for Moen. We hustled from the airport to the office of Inco Homes in Upland. I had everything staged and ready. As I parked, my brain started racing.

Because I feared we would be late, I was in rush mode.

Bill stopped me. "Slow down young fellow, you only have one opportunity to make a first impression!" He then ran down a checklist of necessary items we would need for the sales call. Fortunately, I had all of them. When all was said and done, we weren't late and our compelling presentation convinced the purchasing agent to specify our product.

The point, of course, was to be ready. Really ready! Customers make fun of me because I invariably have a 'Sig List' which is no more than a list of items to be discussed, questions to ask, and points to make.

Another thing that makes me the target of ridicule is "Sig Time", defined as arriving to an appointment well ahead of the appointed time. My rule of thumb is 15 minutes!

Because many things in our lives are not within our control, "Sig Time" creates a buffer that makes a prompt arrival more likely.

Preparation is essential. Because in business, surprises are usually bad, the Reputable Rep working with a factory manager needs to prepare them for possible questions or issues the customer may bring up. The Reputable Rep should give the factory manager insight into the thinking of the customer: likes, dislikes, or status of pertinent open items.

I remember talking to a distributor owner about scheduling a meeting with a factory national sales manager that the owner knew all too well. His comment to me, "I know I'm an important customer for your factory and that you are required to bring him in here to see me, but make sure he doesn't say anything stupid!"

The Reputable Rep adeptly balances the personalities in the territory.

Can he prevent a factory guy from saying something stupid?

Probably not, but good preparation will increase the likelihood of a productive sales call. In a scenario like this, it's best to discuss a well-structured sales call that leaves little room for an off-the-cuff stupid statement.

SIMPLE MARKETING

Going to war in the industrial sales business need not be complicated. The Reputable Rep has a knack for simplifying the complex.

In 1993, I became the independent rep for Bradford White, a virtual unknown brand in the West at that time. Working closely with the entire management team, but primarily with Carmen Catania, we established a plan to set up a network of distributors to cover the territory.

A map of Southern California stapled to a peg board was hung above the desk in my garage. Pins were placed on the locations of potential distributors and their branches. I kept adding pins until all of the market was covered. That became the target list. The plan was to sell Bradford White to those distributors; a simple plan that would need much more detail, but was the foundation of the product launch. Believe it or not, the crazy plan actually worked!

PART 4

SALES STRATEGIES

THE 'WHAT IF' GAME

Smart reps employ this strategy to move a conversation from nowhere to somewhere. Example: "What if I were able to provide you a product that has the features the market demands while at the same time putting you in a position to increase your margins?"

One of my favorite stories concerning the value of the *What If* game follows:

A husband and wife are having a serious conversation:

Wifey: If I was to die, would you remarry?

Hubby: Well, you know I would be really upset, but I would hate living alone, so yes, I think in time, if you were to die, I would remarry.

Wifey: If I was to die and you remarried, would you let your new wife live in our house?

Hubby: Well, it's a nice house. I'd hate to move. So, I suppose if you were to die that I'd let my new wife live in this house.

Wifey: If I was to die and you remarried and your new wife lived in our house, would you let her drive my car?

Hubby: Well, I suppose so.

Wifey: Would you let her use my golf clubs?

Hubby: Of course not! She's left handed!

The moral of the story is you just never know what can be learned by playing the What If game!

CREATING DEMAND

Creating demand for a manufacturer's product in the secondary market is the mission of every Reputable Rep. It's the ground game that will dictate success or failure.

Early in my career, after investing substantial capital and floor space for my product, I was challenged by the owner of a major wholesaler.

"This warehouse is not a museum! Your product better have buyers eager to buy! If not, our next conversation will be different!"

When seen in the market as a product influencer driving business, the Reputable Rep becomes a sales consultant.

"The unique aspect of a Reputable Rep and what makes them so successful is their ability to combine two critical factors to the end-user, the contractor. First, the relationship: Trust is a critical factor for a contractor. By choosing to install your products, he is taking on the liability associated with the product and the installation. The Reputable Rep has earned the contractor's trust. Given the turnover involved in a direct sales organization, that trust is invaluable.

Secondly, the bundle: The Reputable Rep has a cohesive, complementary line card of offerings that create a bundled-solution, enabling the contractor to have a one-stop shop experience. One source for training, education, service, problem solving, and warranty!"

— **Jeff Davis, VP Wholesale Sales, Reliance Worldwide**

TWO HALVES EQUAL A WHOLE

Sometimes decision influencers are vague about their product preferences. They don't want to wander to the edge of a limb all by themselves. In this case, the Reputable Rep can use the play I call, *Two Halves Equal a Whole*. Here's how it works.

The rep has a meeting about a specific product with a sub-contractor. He asks the sub-contractor friend if he will use the product on a specific, upcoming job, provided the builder approves it. Not wanting to be difficult with a rep that can be counted on to help him out of jams, the sub-contractor, of course, agrees. That's the first half of the whole. The rep then meets with the builder to discuss the benefits of having the rep's product on the job. When the builder wavers, the rep mentions that the sub-contractor is on board.

Not wanting to have a conflict with the sub-contractor, the builder agrees to put the product on the job. That's the second half of the whole. *Two Halves* just added up to a whole bunch of business! This strategy also works when a clever rep walks a job during construction to snoop out sales opportunities with labor-savings products he sells. The Reputable Rep takes pictures of the opportunities to save the contractor money. He then tracks down the plumber on the job to discuss the opportunity and get him on board. When he agrees, the rep has converted half of the whole. The second half occurs when the rep goes to the contractor's home office to discuss the opportunity with the decision makers. Armed with the photo and the endorsement from the plumber on the job, the second half of the whole is put into play and the sale is the logical result.

When *Two Halves Equal a Whole* is executed, the Reputable Rep has connected the dots to success.

THE HIT AND RUN

In the wholesale distribution business, a hit and run occurs when a factory man, manufacturer's rep, or wholesaler sales person identifies a business opportunity, pounces on it, and closes the deal, by hook or by crook. Down the road when a problem arises, that salesperson does a Houdini vanishing act. Phone calls aren't returned, e-mails go unanswered, and texts are ignored. This is a bit of an exaggeration, but not as far-fetched as you might think. The Reputable Manufacturer's Representative understands that service and attention to issues is far more important than making the sale.

While managing the moving parts involved in securing a sale on a project, always remember that the order is the beginning of the process, not the end of it. When you strategically employ *Two Halves Equal a Whole*, make certain that your product for that job is delivered promptly, installed properly, and works as advertised! I've seen scores of hit and run people accidentally find our secret industry. Fortunately, they don't last, but all too often they are replaced with other hit and run operators.

STORY TIME: DESERT HORIZONS

I implemented the Two Halves Equal a Whole strategy on a huge country club project in Palm Desert in 1980. Yes, that was a long time ago, but the sales principle still applies today. The job was called Desert Horizons.

Bulldozers shaped the terrain for the enormous project. A construction trailer was placed on site. As a salesman for Moen, I trained myself to look for clouds of dust resulting from bulldozers grading lots for construction.

Invariably, the job superintendent would be found in the trailer. He would either take the time to talk about the project, or refer me to the home office. In this case 'The Super' made sure I knew that he was the boss and whatever he said, went. I eagerly showed him the sample of Moen's first-ever widespread faucet. Bill O'Neill, a Moen legend, one of my mentors and, at that time, the national builder sales manager, had taught me how to 'pitch' this product. He described the faucet as if he was critiquing a Rembrandt at an art museum. "Marvel at the hint of the baroque and the touch of the rococo."

As 'The Super' and I stood outside on the trailer. Bulldozers created a dust storm that blew dust into our eyes. It was August in the desert.

The sun pounded my body with the force of a sledgehammer, but I uttered not one complaint about the elements. Acting like a wimp in the construction business is another form of rep suicide. Sweat rolled off my head and into my eyes. I called an audible at the line of scrimmage. I scrapped the baroque and the rococo sales pitch and simply told 'The Super' that he had an opportunity to be the first builder in the nation to feature Moen's new faucet. Was he on board? He grumbled, "That spout looks like the head of a cobra snake." I again ignored the baroque and rococo design points and simply replied, "Pretty cool, isn't it?"

After shaking his head skeptically, he proudly told me that he had the power to make the decision, but that he wanted to make sure his plumbing contractor, Bob Ball, was on board. New products could be great, but they could also have an unforeseen installation problem.

I had 'half of the whole'. I showed Bob Ball the widespread faucet.

'The Super' reviewed the product from the top, down. Bob Ball reviewed the it from the bottom, up. "As usual, Moen engineering is making the installation pretty easy for my guys. Tell 'The Super' if he's on board, I'm on board." Mission accomplished! Two halves equaled a whole! The project, completed 35 years ago, still stands proudly at the corner of HWY 111 and Cook Street in Palm Desert. The order would be for 250 kitchen faucets, 500 tub shower valves and 1,000 widespread lavatory faucets.

I quietly celebrated! I would be the first salesman in the country to sell the widespread faucet that featured a touch of baroque and a hint of rococo.

The order was shipped through my distributor, Familian. The project started on schedule.

The faucets were installed easily; just as advertised. Now for the surprise! The home office builder marketing people walked through the model homes in utter dismay. "That... without question is the ugliest faucet we've ever seen!"

'The Super' called me in full panic mode. The handles were okay, but that cobra spout had to go! I called Moen's home office in Elyria, Ohio. The only solution was to ship more conventional looking spouts from their Waltec division in Canada. They were air-freighted directly to my house.

As soon as the shipment arrived I opened the first box of spouts. They were cosmetically fine, but installation would be a huge problem! Because the threads on the spout shank had burrs, in order to accept the mounting nut, they would need to be scrubbed with a wire brush. OUCH!

I spent the next two weeks on the job with a crew of plumbers in a scorching desert heatwave. We replaced the cobra spouts that featured the baroque and rococo and were a dream to install with conventionally designed spouts that were aesthetically acceptable to the builder, but were a nightmare for the me, the 'Super', and the plumber.

After the Desert Horizons job, 'The Super', thankfully, disappeared, but the plumber went on to do other projects in the desert, and all of them were Moen!

THE CLEVER SALES ANGLE

> "The Reputable Rep is creative when their hands are tied by the manufacturer."
>
> — **Fred Laube, Director of Corporate Operations, Hirsch Pipe and Supply**

THE RIGHT FIT

As a rep desperate to attract factories to my line card, I took on an unknown faucet line that was not an 'A' or 'B' line and had no stocking distributors. However, since I was a faucet guy, it was worth a try.

I focused on the positives: it was a good product, manufactured in the U.S., and not sold at retail.

I set-up a meeting with a large repair plumbing contractor who was purchasing Bradford White, a factory that operated with the same basic principles. My relationship with the buyer and owner of the repair company certainly helped.

In this scenario, Larry plays the part of the salesman and Enrique plays the part of the buyer. The conversation starts with pleasantries and a brief product review before escalating:

Larry: What faucets are you currently stocking on your trucks?

Enrique: We carry a variety of brands.

Larry: Why don't you simplify matters by carrying one brand?

Enrique: Because of the bins in our trucks.

Larry: So you have chosen products that fit into your bins?

Enrique: Exactly!

Larry: No brand has a complete offering that fits into all your bins?

Enrique: Right again!

Larry: What if my line of faucets were offered to you in boxes that would fit your bins?

Enrique: Based on the samples I'm looking at, you've got the same problem.

Larry: Let me measure your bins, talk to the factory about providing boxes that fit your bins, and get back to you.

The moral of the story: The factory, although reluctantly, actually agreed to the request and a deal was made.

PART 5

SALES BY SEGMENT

NEW CONSTRUCTION

The products installed in residential and commercial projects travel a similar route. They are manufactured, sold through a network of factory sales people and or manufacturer's reps to wholesale distributors, and ultimately to contractors who install them. The competition is fierce.

There are many people that influence product decisions. Price is always an important factor, but is not the only consideration.

Here's a list of key product influencers in the supply chain:

1. **Distributors**. Wholesale distributors aligned with particular manufacturers can sway product selection with their loyal sub-contractors who are eager to support them and the products they endorse.

2. **Sub-Contractors**. Personal experiences, good or bad, that sub-contractors, such as plumbers and mechanicals, have with particular products can be a big part of the final decision. In today's market, there is an increasingly popular negotiating ploy called 'value engineering' where sub-contractors have a greater influence in selecting products that will allow a project to pencil in 'at or below' budget.

3. **Specifying Engineers**. They have a critical impact

because they author the rules of engagement: specifying the product or the criteria for a product they will approve. Open specs allow for alternative products provided that the products meet specific requirements. Closed specs are rare, but if they are in play, will spell out criteria that only one manufacturer can meet.

4. **Builders/General Contractors**. Depending on the project, they can play hardball, overriding every other influencer. In some cases, that works to their advantage. In others, it may backfire. Delivery problems can stall projects. Quality issues, product certification/building code hiccups, or incorrect applications can lead to a job nightmare. When these kinds of problems arise, the general contractor or builder playing hardball can blame no one but themselves, which hits them hard in the wallet.

5. **Architects**. Products that can influence the size of rooms or will require provisions for chimneys or vents may require architect involvement. An example would be a whirlpool tub that is 'special' in its size or configuration.

REBATES

This is the WILDCARD. I call it, 'Feeding the Cartel'. Distributors negotiate programs with factories that provide them with extra discounts, but sub-contractors and builders can be swayed by a competing factory's incentives that go directly to them.

MANAGING THE MOVING PARTS

In today's market, the Reputable Rep is best equipped to create product consensus by working with all of these decision influencers. The obvious place to start is at the drawing board. For commercial jobs, that's the specifying engineer. For residential jobs, it's the builder. But believing a product will ultimately be purchased because it is specified is akin to believing in the Easter Bunny. It's a start, but only a start. Managing the moving parts is paramount. The Reputable Rep understands that. He will work his way up and down the supply chain to insure his product is purchased.

> "From my perspective, The Reputable Rep must have the ability to cover all segments: distribution, contractor, and engineer. Another important factor, particularly in the residential market, is the end-user/consumer. The advent of the internet has prompted the consumer to do extensive research when selecting a product. Social media can make or break a product line. To prevent issues from going viral, potential problems downstream must be addressed promptly!"
>
> **— John Warner, Director of Sales, Laars**

As John says, being a complete Reputable Rep who manages all the moving parts in the supply chain with a sense of urgency is the key. The philosophy that 'Problems are Opportunities' wins the day.

REPAIR AND REMODEL

The repair remodel business is far less glamorous than the new construction segment. There are very few 80-yard touchdown passes to be had on in this side of the business. Three yards and a cloud of dust is the norm. But…and this is a huge 'BUT'…this side of the business represents the lion's share of the business. Example: There are approximately 9 million water heaters sold every year. An average new construction year in the U.S. produces roughly 1 million homes. That's 1 million water heaters. Bottom line, 8 out of 9 water heaters are sold in the replacement market. It's true that many products that reps sell are skewed the other way.

Products like ABS and PVC pipe are heavily involved in new construction.

Other categories might be mixed 50/50. Any way you slice it, the repair remodel segment must not be ignored. In this discussion we'll talk about wholesaler counter business, multi-truck repair plumbers, and luxury products sold through showrooms.

Rep agencies typically do not target Maintenance/Repair/Operations distributors (MROs) like Grainger and HD Maintenance Supply. Because of that, I'm setting them aside. Likewise, big box/hardware stores are not part of our discussion.

The Repair/Remodel Dynamic:

Calling on repair plumbers represents a sizeable challenge for distributors, manufacturer's reps, and factory sales people alike.

Depending on the market, repair/remodel (R&R) plumbers might outnumber new-work plumbers by 30 to 50 fold. Many R&R plumbers work out of their homes, making rep sales calls difficult. Because of that, most manufacturer's reps carve out a generous amount of time at city counters, particularly with wholesalers marketing primarily to this sector. Understanding the critical importance of this side of the business, Signature Sales recently added a rep whose sole function is calling on multi-truck service and repair plumbers. The goal, of course, is education; educating the R&R contractors on the variety of products represented that could benefit them in their businesses. To be successful in the repair market it is critical for the rep to be aligned with the distributors that keep their counters busy!

SHOWROOMS

Follow the bouncing ball. National distributors, particularly Ferguson, have made it a priority to expand their showroom business. I'm guessing they've spent lots of money analyzing this segment. They've figured out that it's trending higher and higher. My advice: follow the bouncing ball. It's likely filled with opportunities and sales dollars.

Like all business segments, there are challenges. Sometimes the key associates are on the phone or with a client. Patience is an agonizing virtue. While waiting, Reputable Reps attend to phone calls, texts, and e-mails.

Carry Windex and paper towels in your car. Making the products you have on display look 'spiffy' will separate you from the herd of sales people that hit and run. Demonstrate to the showroom people that you will go the extra mile to help them. And...train...train...train. Train sales people how to read your catalog. Ram home the features and benefits of your product that help them close a sale. Train them in the art of selling, and just as important, sell them on you. Hit and run sales people are also prevalent in showrooms.

If you're easy to reach and eager to solve problems, you've got a leg up on the competition. Service what you sell.

That may include talking to the showroom's homeowner customer or even going to a jobsite or home. Get custom builder and designer leads from your showroom friends. Creating demand for your products will help the showroom and help you! Don't take a half in, half out approach. Either commit to the showroom business or get out of it. Lack of commitment is a waste of your time and the customer's!

> "I was expanding my plumbing business to include a line of appliances. I met with a rep I'll call 'Mr. Big', who represented the incumbent vendor. Mr. Big told me we needed to support his product exclusively. Then he bluntly asked, 'If I provide this product to you, what will you do for us?' That was the conclusion of a short meeting!
>
> I then met with a second vendor in the same product category. He started the conversation with, 'Here's what I'm going to do for you!' He told me it would not be in my best interest to be sole sourced. We worked together to develop a business plan that was good for both of us!"
>
> **— Gregg Ferguson, Ferguson Enterprises**

STORY TIME: SAVING WATER

My dearly departed friend Tim Samut worked for me for many years.

He was the master of asking smart questions that would sniff out huge sales opportunities. In addition to being a dear, dear friend, he had a nose for business, an ability to recognize sales opportunities, and a gift for finding a hidden treasure beneath a rock.

Timmy was in the central coast doing a counter day. One of his featured products was the Laing recirculating pump. A non-descript man (Mr. Cambria) came to the counter and picked Timmy's brain about the ins and outs of the pump's operation and installation. Timmy pressed Mr. Cambria to explain why he was so interested. Mr. Cambria gave Timmy a business card and told him to drop by his office at his convenience.

It was well publicized that the city of Cambria was struggling with a water shortage. Timmy never underestimated an opportunity, and this sales call was no different. He solicited the help of Bob Hutslar, Laing's national sales manager, who joined him at the meeting. The population of Cambria was about 6,000 at the time. Since a great deal of cold water goes down the drain while people wait for hot water for their showers and dishwashing, Mr. Cambria determined that it would make sense to install Laing Auto-Circ recirculating pumps into every home in town. The city hired a team of plumbers to do the installations.

The order was for over 3,000 pumps—a sale for over $500,000! And yes, the order was shipped through wholesale distribution! Bottom line: keep your ears open, ask smart questions, and connect the dots that separate opportunity and success!

STORYTIME: THE GAS COMPANY

Sadly, sales people walk past sales opportunities daily without recognizing them. They lack clear vision! They lack creativity, curiosity, or both.

> "Of all the characteristics we look for in choosing a member of our team, curiosity is probably most important. It is also one of the best indicators of success."
>
> — **Bruce Carnevale, Executive Vice President and COO, Bradford White Corporation**

When I was in the distribution business, I was will-calling water heaters I needed for a customer. On the way back to the office, I happened to pass by the gas company in Santa Fe Springs.

I wondered what I might be able to sell them. How about water heaters?

Since the gas company lights pilots for appliances, maybe they provide or sell them as well. This turned out to be the coldest of cold calls that turned into the biggest of big deals.

With my truck full of water heaters in the parking lot and dressed like a truck driver (jeans and tennis shoes) I walked through the front door of the giant utility to do some fact finding. I was shuffled around from person to person until I met a secretary who gave me a hot tip, "You should talk to Elsa. She's in the market for water heaters, big time!" I was directed to another building where Elsa was located. I walked into a side, unlocked door. The first person I met directed me to Elsa's office.

I gave her my business card, shook her hand, and said, "I understand you're in the market for water heaters."

Her response was amazing and shocking. "Oh my goodness, you must be a mind reader! I've been wondering where in the world I could purchase large quantities and get them quickly."

I was baffled. "How many are you looking for?" She smiled. "200 a week for the next 10 weeks."

I was mystified. "Really?"

"Oh yes, we have a new program I'm administrating. We will be providing free water heaters to any family who is economically needy, living beneath the poverty line. The response has been phenomenal. We'll run out of funding well before we run out of applicants.

"Please send me a quotation for your 30 and 40 gallon gas models.

Last year's program was for wall furnaces.

"This year, it's water heaters. We already have agreements with licensed contractors to do the installations."

"I'm heading to the office right now and will have a quote to you this afternoon!"

"Perfect. I'll review it!"

After returning to the office, I faxed her a competitive quote. The following morning, I had purchase orders in hand for 200 water heaters a week for the next 4 weeks.

That was the beginning of a beautiful relationship!

After reading this story, you're probably saying, "I don't think so, Sig!" The absolute reality is that this story is 100% true! Unbelievable? Yes! But, nonetheless, 100% true.

Was I lucky? Absolutely! But what I've learned in my career is that the harder I work, the luckier I get. The Reputable Rep lives by this adage.

PART 6

THE HUMAN ELEMENT

THE WELL-LIKED REP

Reps that are well-liked are not necessarily effective reps. I've known many reps who are very well-liked, but for a number of reasons are not able to leverage their popularity into concrete business. Well-liked reps say the right things and are agreeable. They find it impossible to say no! What gets them into trouble is saying yes when the real answer is no. Then, when the rubber meets the road and the customer finds out, usually by accident, that the answer is no, a lack of respect for Mr. Yes occurs. Because he is such a nice guy, customers don't confront Mr. Yes.

They just quietly take their business elsewhere. Mr. Yes is very popular at all industry functions and never misses a golf tournament.

He goes out of his way to shake every hand and say nice things about everyone. He is the Will Rogers protégé who never met a man he didn't like. However, because substance, respect, and honesty are critical in life and the business world, Mr. Yes does not deliver much business.

STORY TIME: GOOD-TIME CHARLIE

My lifelong friend and mentor, Carmen, was an engineer before making the move into the rep business. Shortly after the career change, his partner had a massive heart attack, leaving Carmen to run a business he knew little about. He scrambled and restructured. He was determined to keep the business afloat until, hopefully, his partner, recovered. He focused on getting his arms around the business. Carmen's plan would include firing an unproductive salesman I'll call Good-Time Charlie. Since he would be making sales calls on Charlie's accounts, Carmen prepared sales reports for every customer he had inherited. He walked into Charlie's favorite account and introduced himself. The customer went far beyond the call of duty to talk about what a great guy Charlie was, how reliable he was, what a ray of sunshine he was, and how much he would be missed.

Carmen, ever the realist, pulled out his sales report and commented, "Mr. Customer, let me get this straight, you really like Charlie?"

"Absolutely! Charlie was our favorite rep! We love Charlie!"

Carmen, as is his style, got to the heart of the matter. "I'm looking at sales reports for every one of our lines. You didn't buy anything from Charlie. Please do me a big favor, like me less and start buying more!"

THE GAMES PEOPLE PLAY

"In my younger sales days, tearing up the San Diego market for Hamilton Supply, my competitor, Jerry Grosslight from Familian, offered me a job. Not to work for them, but to simply stay home!"

— **Louie Armstrong, Ferguson Enterprises**

Before Ferguson's arrival to the West Coast, Familian was regarded as the wholesale leader in Southern California. Uncle Jerry Grosslight was 'THE MAN'! The buyer was 'King Bob'.

Here's a note from Gary Grosslight about his Uncle Jerry, who worked hard to offset the mind games of 'King Bob' even though Jerry Grosslight was 'THE MAN'!

"It was pitiful how 'King Bob', Familian's buyer, treated factory people and reps alike. The vendors would sometimes arrive for an early morning appointment and still be in the waiting room well into the afternoon.

On the other hand, Uncle Jerry always made time for reps and factory people. He understood the value of these relationships. Uncle Jerry taught us the importance of encouraging teamwork with our vendor partners, particularly manufacturer's reps who live and die in the local market."

— Gary Grosslight, Ferguson Enterprises

LIFE ON THE ROAD

I'm certain that everyone reading this book has a hair-raising story about life on the road in the challenging world of industrial sales. This one, from my friend Tom Schoendorf, is a classic.

"I was in the air the morning of September 11, 2001, flying from NYC to Memphis, Tennessee. When I got off the plane and started walking through the terminal, I failed to notice that everything was being shut down: stores, restaurants, etc. Once I got to curbside, I hooked up with my rep who was astonished to see me. 'I can't believe you made it!' I was surprised, 'Why? My flight is on time.'

The rep continued, 'Terrorists are hijacking planes and crashing them into buildings. All the airports are being shut-down!' I turned on my cell phone. I had 10 voicemails. My wife Chris was worried sick about me and so were my colleagues and friends. As the day moved on we began to realize the incredible toll it was taking on our great country. After our meeting at FedEx Corporate, in Memphis, I rented a car and started the 36-hour drive home to Long Island. There were no planes in the sky, but the roads were packed with travelers like me, trying to get home. As I approached the George Washington Bridge from New Jersey to New York late at night, I remember looking at the NYC skyline and thinking that without the Twin Towers, it would forever look different. I've saved my plane ticket and still have it in my desk!"

— **Tom Schoendorf, Highland Tank**

PART 7

THE REPUTABLE REP

RELATIONSHIPS

> "I love to see reps! When they're with me, they're not with my competitors!"
>
> **— Louie Armstrong, Ferguson Enterprises**

The Reputable Rep, like the distributors and contractors in his market, has both a financial and personal interest in the people he or she does business with. Reputable Reps can be the glue that cements factory-customer loyalty.

> "The Reputable Rep forges relationships that provide an entree for sales managers to develop partnerships and negotiate programs with decision makers."
>
> **— Joe Cicora, National Sales Manager, Red White Valve**

My friend Bill Glockner weighs in on the Reputable Rep-manufacturer-distributor triangle.

> "The Reputable Rep promotes the development of long-lasting, supportive relationships with the rep's manufacturers."
>
> — **Bill Glockner, President, Hirsch Pipe and Supply**

In the sales business, there are careers that demand a one-time sale mentality; a hit and run. To be successful in this arena, an aggressive strategy is used.

The result of this tactic has opposing reactions from the unsuspecting prospective buyer: succumbing to the pressure or walking away. Car dealerships live or die with the hit and run sales approach.

Because it is a relationship business, the mentality of the rep in the industrial sales business is altogether different. Over time, Reputable Reps and customers become friends. The essence of the relationship is trust and respect. Reputable Rep-customer relationships can last a lifetime.

> "The Reputable Rep cares more about building long-lasting relationships than the big sale!"
>
> — **Steve Shipley, Hirsch Pipe and Supply**

These relationships are shared with manufacturers, not deferred to them.

"It drives me nuts when a rep abdicates his relationship with the customer and allows the manufacturer to 'own' the relationship. When that occurs, what value does the rep have to the manufacturer? Like all things in our business, it's a balance. There should be an appropriate relationship between the customer and the manufacturer. The Reputable Rep fosters this, and guides it, but doesn't abdicate it (or let it be taken) completely by the manufacturer."

— Bruce Carnevale, Executive Vice President and COO, Bradford White Corporation

THE BALANCING ACT

"At first glance, the life of a Reputable Rep looks easy and glamorous. Nothing is further from the truth! Early mornings, late nights, 24/7 availability, coddling customers, and meeting the high demands of their manufacturers who all have different agendas. Reporting requirements, demands on the reps' time and different cultures—make it very difficult to navigate and manage!!!"

— Mark Taylor, Executive VP and General Manager, Bradford White Corporation

Reputable Reps are like tightrope walkers. The key is balance. They balance the factory customer relationship, ensuring neither party has an unfair advantage. The Reputable Rep balances their call activity to ensure they are both servicing distributors and creating new business for them.

They must also balance the time spent on the lines they represent.

> "A manufacturer asks his manufacturer's representative, 'How can I get more of your agency's time selling my product?' The reply was, 'My agency devotes 20 man-hours a week to your line. Five hours of that time we spend selling your product and the other 15 we spend chasing backorders, correcting pricing, and fixing product issues.'"
>
> **— Joe Maiale, VP Sales, InSinkErator**

Another challenge for the Reputable Rep is balancing the needs of competing distributors in the territory. The Reputable Rep has experience and expertise to navigate these waters honestly.

> "Being a vendor representative is a tough job! Dealing with competing wholesalers and dealing with competing contractors is challenging! I always appreciate it when I can trust that somebody is being honest and just giving me the facts so I can make the best decision!"
>
> **— Mike Lorber, Ferguson Enterprise**

The owner, of Firefighter Gas Safety Products, Tod Minato weighs in on the Reputable Rep's balancing act.

"From my perspective, a Reputable Rep knows how to walk a tightrope. There is a conflict in every deal he puts together. He makes his living (commission) selling my product, but he has to put a good deal together for the customer because he represents the customer as well. The list of customers that a rep has a good relationship with is what attracts manufactures to his organization. If a deal is skewed in the favor of one party or the other, the rep can hurt an ally. The reason I have stayed with Signature Sales so long is because they take the right approach of promoting fairness. To me, a deal is a transaction that either party would be willing to be on either side of. Looking for an edge on a deal is natural, but should not take priority over fairness and integrity. When a rep fails to see the complexity of representing both sides of a deal, it makes me uncomfortable."

— **Tod Minato, President, Firefighter Gas Safety Products**

"Above all a Reputable Rep must demonstrate integrity with both his distributor and vendor partners. This can prove difficult as it means keeping secrets for each. In the end, the rep has to know what is right and work to ensure it is achieved."

— **Bill Glockner, President/CEO, Hirsch Pipe and Supply**

TEAMWORK

I've said many times that great teamwork makes a task feel like it's not really work at all!

> "Reputable Reps believe in their lines and promote them. They work with us as a team to make it a success!"
>
> — **John Potter, Ferguson Enterprise**

A Reputable Rep who acts as a skilled middleman between the contractor and the distributor is a huge asset to any wholesaler's team.

There are many times, when the rep is the glue that holds together the contractor-distributor relationship.

Over time these 'team wins' earn trust and respect. They insure an audience for multi-line reps with other products they are marketing.

> "Reputable Reps have honest conversations with us. Over time, a relationship is built that makes it easy to support the lines they represent."
>
> — **Fred Laube, Director of Corporate Operations, Hirsch Pipe and Supply**

THE RIGHT REP

Does the factory make the rep or does the rep make the factory? This question is the business equivalent of the old chicken and egg question. I'll argue that success occurs when the Reputable Rep and the factory meet the truck halfway.

When the spirit of compromise and an unwavering commitment to succeed are established as top priorities, it's a WIN-WIN!

In our business, every rep is not a fit for every line and no factory is a fit for every rep. The key is the fit:

- Alignment on marketing strategy
- Ample manpower
- Secondary market synergy
- Personality

When these components gel, marketing magic has an opportunity to occur!

"Many years ago, I met a rep through AIM/R. He did not carry my product line, but I liked his style and his approach to business. He was located in a market my company was struggling in. After concluding that our current rep was not the right fit, I approached this rep about representing our line. His business was well north of $100M in sales. Since our line was worth less than $1M in his territory, I was pleasantly surprised that he expressed interest. More conversation led to the understanding and appreciation of our vision. He agreed we had a strong go-to-market strategy and that the product would sell with the right partner. We talked candidly about what was required to grow the market: a painful change on our end and a significant investment on his. We agreed to trust each other and make the commitments, investments, and changes needed. Within 5 years, that rep was selling nearly $30M of our products in the same territory! My conclusion: Entering a partnership with a committed rep agency with the right fit can yield great results!"

— Jeff Davis, VP Wholesale sales, Reliance Worldwide

SUCCESSION PLAN

> "Without a doubt, the biggest issue we see with reps is the lack of a strong succession plan. Because there are many unique challenges in the rep business, succession planning can be difficult. The best resource available is networking with reps who have been successful at executing their succession plan."
>
> **— Bruce Carnevale, Executive Vice President and COO,**
> **Bradford White Corporation**

In the early years of Signature Sales, at about the time I finally began to see light at the end of a long tunnel, my mentor and lifelong friend, Carmen Catania, told me I needed a succession plan. I remember boldly replying, "Are you out of your mind? I don't even know if my business will still be viable in 5 years, one year or even tomorrow." Carmen was not deterred!

He kept reminding me…and reminding me. I'm happy to say that this hardheaded German finally listened. Shortly after we entered the new millennium, our plan was put in place and ultimately executed.

If you are the principal of a rep firm, I implore you to take Carmen's advice. Ensure long term viability of your agency. Reputable Reps discuss long-term planning, business savvy, and succession plans when interviewing for top lines.

> "The rep must have a plan for growth, sustainability, and succession. Without a plan for addressing the future, the agency will eventually fold or be absorbed."
>
> **— Mark Taylor, Executive VP and General Manager, Bradford White Corporation**

REPUTABLE REPS AS 'GO GIVERS'

I've shared a wonderful book called *The Go Giver* with many friends, including 'Mr. Go-Giver', Joe Notte.

> "I stopped by Joe's office and saw a little book called The Go Giver. After sarcastically asking Joe if he was reading it or if he wrote it, he said, 'Sig sent it to me'. So, of course, I read it! The book delivers a very simple message for life and business: Always do the 'right thing' without expecting anything in return. I would add that doing the right thing is certainly not the same thing as doing the easy thing. Sometimes doing the right thing involves stressing a relationship, which can be a challenge for most people, but especially sales people."
>
> **— Bruce Carnevale, Executive Vice President and COO, Bradford White Corporation**

Success in the business world is the by-product of doing the right thing.

> "A Reputable Rep is the guy that can walk that fine line that separates distributors in the same market. The best example is a close friend of mine who worked for Kohler for many years. Even though he has two family members working for competitors, he's always been able to separate right from wrong. It's a talent that not all reps have been able to execute."
>
> **— Steve Grosslight, Ferguson Enterprises**

PRICING, COMPETITION, AND CREATIVITY

> "A Reputable Rep knows when to say 'no'!"
>
> **— Bob Berumen, Hirsch Pipe and Supply**

The biggest mistake a rep can make is to focus solely on price. Many studies have proven, over and over again, that price is not the number one reason a customer moves on to a different rep or supplier.

More important considerations are relationships, service levels, product quality, and product demand/acceptance.

But it would be naïve to say that pricing is not critical. It's a competitive world and purchasers are always weighing value propositions. Having a clever angle is a good way to tackle the pricing conundrum.

Louie Armstrong has a history of finding clever angles to address pricing challenges.

> "Years ago, I called on a plumbing contractor who was in the market for three truckloads of ABS pipe (a $60,000 order). To close the deal, I brought with me an official, printed price sheet from the manufacturer with my actual cost…and a pair of dice. I knew from past experience that the order, if it went out for bid, would be awarded to a distributor that bid 1½-2% over cost. So, I proposed a deal that the contractor agreed to. He would roll the dice. The sum of the numbers rolled would be discounted 50%. If he rolled a 4 and a 5, the sum would be 9, discounted 50%, he would be marked up 4½%. If he rolled snake-eyes, he would be marked up 1%. Even though the math and odds were in my favor the contractor proceeded because it was fun. He rolled two sixes and the order was priced at 6% over cost!"
>
> **— Louie Armstrong, Ferguson Enterprises**

SENSE OF URGENCY

> "Reputable Reps answer their cellphones. Most reps screen calls!"
>
> **— John Potter, Ferguson Enterprise**

In this, the era of e-mails, texts, and other electronic instant messaging, it amazes me that the most common complaint customers have is slow response time from factories and reps. I've said many times that the thing I like best about being a rep is that an average guy with a sense of urgency can be regarded as a superstar of sorts.

The response time for good news phone calls in the

industrial sales business is typically good. Problem calls are a different animal altogether. The percentage of reps that consistently returns calls promptly when faced with issues to resolve or problems to solve is dreadfully low.

These reps have not learned that problems are opportunities in disguise. Problems that arise provide opportunities for the rep to demonstrate value. Problem calls can trigger one of the following plays.

A. Delegating: It is not unusual for reps to call their go-to person in the office to resolve a customer problem. I call this 'Depositing a turd into someone else's mailbox.' When this tool is in a rep's playbook, it matters not that the recipient's mailbox is already full of turds.

B. Shifting into neutral: This is the classic case of rep paralysis culminating into 'The Stall'. The rep that stalls hopes that by some miracle the problem will magically go away. Stalls might be caused by the rep's factory using 'The Stall' on them. There are many reasons or excuses for factory and rep stalls. The most common, real or not, are 'traveling' or 'in a meeting'. Reps employing 'The Stall' rationalize that it is fruitless to return a customer's call without a resolution.

C. Taking care of it NOW! The Reputable Rep has a different mindset. He consistently returns calls, with either good news or bad news. It is a top priority. Here's an example of a Reputable Rep returning a problem call: "I am so, so sorry about this issue. Please understand that I will do everything in my power to get it resolved. I've left a message for the factory's regional manager. In the meanwhile, I'm looking at other options. I know that when I hurt you, I hurt your customer as well. If it would help ease your pain, I would be happy to call your plumbers being harmed."

All customers demand swift resolution of urgent issues. That's a given. However, the advantage that the Reputable Rep has is that he understands his customer.

I had a thirty-year relationship with the owner of a large independent distributor who had zero tolerance for problems. When he called, not only did I interrupt whatever I was doing to answer his call, I committed to resolving the issue eyeball to eyeball. If at all possible, I would rearrange my schedule to be in his office the same day or the next morning. I would walk into his office and he would start the conversation exactly like this:

"Sig, you didn't have to drop everything and come out here to see me!"

I would just smile. Then he would let me have it, getting everything off his chest. I would simply reply, "You are absolutely right!"

"So you agree with me?"

"Yes, sir!"

"Well what in the hell are you going to do about it?"

"I'll fix it!"

After this initial plea for help, he never asked how I would fix it but felt confident that I would. He typically closed the conversation with this: "Thanks a million. I can always count on you!"

Needless to say, it's not always smart to drop everything to answer the phone. We would be largely ineffective and in some cases rude if this was standard practice. However, a Reputable Rep picks his spots. He establishes priorities.

In the above scenario, fixing the problem wasn't always easy. But once we worked our way through the face to face exercise, with a little give and take, things always seemed to work out. The outbursts were not common, perhaps quarterly, but when they did reoccur, our business relationship turned another notch tighter.

I remember, around lunchtime, popping in on this customer to deliver a requested job quote. I started the conversation, "You wanna grab a quick sandwich?"

"I'd love to, but I've got a factory man from Chicago on his way to my office to take me to lunch."

"No worries, I'll call you to schedule our next meeting."

"Hang on a minute, Sig."

He put his Number 2 man on speaker phone. "When the factory man from Chicago arrives, tell him I had something come up. Take him to lunch and fill me in later."

I was happy for me, but obviously embarrassed for the factory man. Nonetheless it underscores the relationships that Reputable Rep's have in the marketplace.

STORY TIME: TWIN SUITCASES

By now, I'm certain my credibility is shot! I keep talking about wonderful, almost unbelievable success stories. I could go into long lengths about all the times I screwed up or struck out, but since this is my book, I won't. Let's face it, the best hitters in baseball make an out 70% of the time. Just to tip the scale a bit, I'll tell you an unbelievable story that was my biggest blunder of all time. After accepting a job with Moen at the ripe age of 25, I was provided an Oldsmobile station wagon and a set of black display cases for use on sales calls.

They looked like ordinary travel suitcases with clasps on both sides, but inside was a black velvet cloth that blanketed faucet samples. I was taught to spread out the velvet as the background for the shiny chrome samples. My boss preached, that placed on the black velvet, the samples looked like fine jewelry. The cases also included a valve cutaway, useful for discussing the heart of every Moen faucet, the cartridge.

While relocating, for the first 3 months as the Moen rep in the inland territory, I spent weeknights in a hotel. It was a late Friday afternoon. I was driven to make that one extra call, even if it meant that traffic would be a killer heading home. I was following up on a lead I had dug up, concerning a new work plumber with lots of work whose house double-teamed as his shop. I got the information at a distributor counter for the price of a donut.

A plumber told me that the shop he worked for only installed Delta faucets. He added that the owner's wife was the real boss and did the purchasing.

I traveled through several back roads before finally arriving. Yes, this was a cold call! With a catalog in one hand and display case in the other, I knocked on the door.

'Mrs. Plumber' invited me into the house/office. I sat across from her at her desk. After breaking the ice, I asked her a question I already knew the answer to, "Is your 'shop brass' Delta?" She confirmed. Then I asked her the thing that I had been trained to do at Moen's sales school, "Does your shop plumb any houses with back-to-back bathrooms?" She responded, "Of course. We specialize in entry level homes and back-to-back is the cheapest way to build affordable housing." I was so glad that this woman knew her stuff.

She had opened the door for a discussion about Moen's ability to rotate the cartridge of the tub shower valve to put the hot and cold piping where it needed to be on both sides of the wall! It could be done without crossing the piping; a big labor and material saver for back-to-back shower installations.

The cutaway would be my silver bullet. I set the case on her desk, flat on its back like a treasure chest. I released the clasps

73

on both sides and slowly opened the case. There were no jewels or gold medallions in my case, nor were there faucet samples. All there was...in full display... was...MY DIRTY LAUNDRY!

The case of the twin suitcases had just been solved and my face was beet red. In a fraction of a second, I was transformed from a man in full control of a conversation to a boy facing his second grade teacher after peeing in his pants.

In retrospect, I'll report to you three positive outcomes:

1. She didn't call the police to report me as a pervert.
2. I learned a valuable lesson: never travel with a personal suitcase that matches a display case.
3. It's possible to recover from even the largest of blunders on record.

After a hardy laugh, she encouraged me to bring in the correct suitcase to show her my prized cutaway.

On that embarrassing Friday afternoon, for some unknown reason, the plumber's wife felt sorry for this knucklehead salesman and changed all of her jobs to Moen.

REPUTABLE REPS AS INNOVATORS

> "Sioux Chief is a line for hands-on reps. It requires a pioneering effort. We look for Reputable Reps who are comfortable on the job site with boots and a hard hat. We look for Reputable Reps who use our breadth of product to find solutions and solve problems for contractors in the field. A Reputable Sioux Chief Rep builds relationships to open doors with distributors, specifying engineers, and contractors. They have integrity and an innovative spirit. Their vehicles are always loaded with samples, that when demonstrated, tell the story of labor-savings."
>
> **— Michael Foster, Sioux Chief**

When it comes to introducing new manufacturers into a market, launching new products of existing manufacturers, or broadening the scope of product offerings to innovating contractors, builders, or distributors, Reliable Reps are the innovation juggernauts. Plumbing reps have become innovators when they sell Timex watches, construction boots, or even bottled water through their wholesale plumbing distributors.

Reps innovate in a market seeking a clever angle to increase sales commissions. Innovating on the front side of these opportunities is the key. If the rep innovator is successful, distributors take note and want to be part of the new market created by the rep. In time the innovated product may become a commodity, driving down prices and commissions. When this occurs, the innovators move on to new innovating products. Innovators are sometimes called 'pioneers' because they are the ones found with an arrow in their back. I, like many reps, have been on the receiving end of arrows that found a home in my back. But the wounds never prevented me from innovating. Signature Sales would not exist today if not for being an innovator with the Bradford White line in 1993. The majority of the lines on Signature's line card were innovating projects that took hold and eventually became preferred products or commodities. My friend Robert Garcia is a human 'Think Tank' thriving in the wholesale business.

"It's all about IDEAS! I love to brainstorm with Reputable Reps to uncover the IDEA that will take my business with that rep to the next level!"

— **Robert Garcia, Plumbing Wholesale Outlet**

This is not to say that all ideas are good and all innovating lines hit a home run. There are far more losers in this game than winners. But that doesn't deter the innovating Reputable Rep who is always up for the challenge. My friend Bob Riggs tells the story of an innovation that flopped.

> "Through the nineties, I worked at Westburne. My boss, Lynn, brought in a line of construction boots sold by his very close friend George, a rep legend who was both a character and an innovator. We had a large selection of the boots at all 14 of our branches. The hope, of course, was that contractors purchasing plumbing supplies at our counters would buy their work boots from us instead of at the shoe store. After 6 months the rep lost the line and our sales were dismal at best. A return of the product was denied. Lynn made it my job to resolve the issue. I accomplished it, not by selling them, but by making them a Christmas present for our employees."
>
> **— Bob Riggs, Winnelson**

INDUSTRY ASSOCIATIONS

All industries have trade organizations. Some thrive; many are in need of a blood transfusion. In plumbing, associations like the PHCC, ASPE, and ASA have local chapters. Many reps get involved in these organizations, but the key is commitment…

> "It's not enough to join an organization! The Reputable Rep is not just involved, he is committed! When an organization loses relevance, the Reputable Rep is the change advocate. When the organization is complacent, he injects it with energy! He owns the organization!
>
> **— Nick Giuffre, President, Bradford White Corporation**

THE BOLD REPUTABLE REP

"Step up or step aside!"

— Kirk Livernash, Signature Sales

The bold Reputable Rep is confident without being cocky. When their customer makes an unfair request, they take the side of the factory; either diplomatically or boldly. Their personal relationship is critical to this strategy. Without it, the bold move should be left beneath the back seat of the car in a locked container! Always remember that the Bold Move is never made arrogantly! In the end, the cocky rep always loses! Sometimes the Reputable Rep makes a bold move with his factory.

STORY TIME: THE LETTER

In the mid-nineties, before e-mail (God-forbid) I made a bold move that I feared would cause me to lose the Bradford White line. We were just beginning to get traction in our market with Bradford White, the new player in the water heater business. But then the inevitable hiccup! Out of nowhere, shipments stretched from mediocre to bad and then to horrible. The wholesalers we had worked hard to get were ready to jump off of the sinking ship...or so they said. I had made pleas up and down the chain of command but not to the very top. Nothing was working!

My bold move, believe it or not, was to send a handwritten plea to Bob Carnevale, President and CEO of Bradford White. My letter pointed out every deficiency in service levels I could muster up.

I was passionate, sincere and unmistakably desperate. I still recall placing the envelope into the mailbox slot and then wishing I had never done it. An equivalent today is that e-mail sent…that really should have been thought through before pushing send.

Ten torturous days later, Carmen, Bradford White's regional manager, called to tell me that Bob was flying into Palm Springs and requested I pick him up from the airport. Knowing well and good that this scenario had the 'Fire the Rep' label written all over it, I was terrified!

I waited at the gate rehearsing my apology, praying I could throw myself to the mercy of the court. Perhaps plead insanity! I awaited his arrival, fidgeting, expecting that surely I was about to be the former rep of the line that kept my fledgling rep company in business.

We made eye contact. He smiled! I trembled! I will never forget his words to me, "Mr. Schmalhofer, I am very surprised to see you here at the airport!" My reply, of course, was that I was picking him up by his request. I braced myself for the other shoe to drop…for my termination! I believed, without question, that this would be the end of my career as a water heater rep, the death of my rep firm, and the unraveling of my life. His reply was slow and confident, "I thought…that perhaps… you were so angry at me…that you wouldn't bother…to pick me up! I received…your heart-tugging letter! I was at the factory…this morning! Everything you said is 100%…on the mark! I've fixed the problem! End…of discussion!"

A critical note to all Reputable Reps: Bold moves are not recommended for the faint-hearted!

THE VERY BOLD MOVE

The next scenario is a contribution from my longtime friend Russ Long, Jr. I'd like to take credit for making this bold move, but in fact it was made by a VP of marketing. I witnessed this bold move and I'll never forget it!

"A great rep is not someone who tells you what you want to hear, but someone who tells you the truth… even when it hurts. We sometimes get caught up in believing we are the best at what we do: from customer service to buying at the best price. A great rep is one who is willing to tell you when you need to STOP negotiating and start working on your own end of the partnership in providing world-class service. I witnessed the epitome of this when I watched a wholesaler make the statement to the vendor 'Come on, look at the discount we are talking about. All I want to do here is at least feel like I am getting laid.' To which the rep replied, 'I know you want to feel like you're getting laid, but I feel like I'm getting screwed!'"

— **Russ Long, Ferguson Enterprises**

After the bold move, time stood still for a torturous interlude, but following that agonizing introspection, a new resolve replaced the ugly exchange and the relationship between the factory and the wholesaler soared—with sales to match!

STORY TIME: ALEXIS PARK

I was a Moen rep in the early eighties when I was summoned by a man I'll refer to as Gunslinger, a plumbing contractor from Las Vegas who was noteworthy for both his loyalty to my product and the handgun strapped in a holster just below his knee. Our meetings were always short and to the point. The answer-machine voicemail I retrieved at 5 PM on a Tuesday, in the summer of 1980, was no different: "I've got a serious problem! Get your ass up here!"

A joke, right? Oh no! Gunslinger never joked or smiled! Ever!

I immediately called him, but it was late, and there was no answer. In those days, there were no pagers, let alone cell phones (ancient times?).

Fearing he would hunt me down and kill me if I failed to respond to his beckoning call, I packed my bag and headed north on interstate 15 to Las Vegas. I checked into the Showboat Hotel (no-longer existing) just before midnight. After a short restless sleep, at 5:45 AM I was at the front door of his shop, which was locked. I went around the back to his yard. When Gunslinger spotted me, he glared angrily, but luckily didn't shoot me. "It's about time! Follow me to the Alexis Park job!"

The Gunslinger had helped me get Moen's recently introduced two-handle tub shower valves on the job. Alexis Park still stands proudly on Harman Avenue. The project was presented to suppliers and contractors as a fast track 496-unit, all-suite hotel that was scheduled to be completed in record time. We went straight to a problem bathroom. He demonstrated the problem. When the tub spout diverter was lifted to divert the water to the shower head, about half the water came out of the spout and about half came out of the shower head. "We just did our water test! I've got the problem with about half of the valves on the job."

I boldly asked, "Is it possible that your plumbers overheated the valves and fried the venturis?"

"Hell no! We're a lot smarter than that!"

Since I needed to buy some time to call the factory, I responded accordingly, "I'll be back after I make some phone calls!"

"While you do that, I'll be out here fixing your screw-up. We need to cut holes in the drywall to pull the valves out!"

"That's fine. I need to inspect as many as possible. I'll be back shortly!" I drove to a truck stop that had pay phones at every table. I ordered breakfast and called Moen's head of engineering. I explained the problem and told him from the looks of it valves were shipped and installed with venturis that were inserted upside down. He responded, "You sound like a typical dumb-ass salesman that doesn't have the faintest idea what he's talking about. It's impossible to insert the venturis upside down. I designed the machine that inserts them! They cannot be inserted upside down by my machine!"

My response, "I'll verify my assessment when I return to the job site. In the meanwhile, I suggest you get on an airplane and see for yourself what I'm dealing with!"

After I crammed down my omelet, I went back to the job.

Gunslinger showed me 36 valves that had been removed. They were not overheated by overzealous soldering by the plumber and they all had upside down Venturis.

To correct the problem, I instructed the Gunslinger to reverse the Venturis and re-install the valves.

The Gunslinger responded, "The labor costs for the drywall man and my men will cost you big time! I'll have my foreman give me a count of problem valves. Your back-charge will be ready when I see you in the morning at six!"

I went back to the truck stop and called my engineer 'friend' again. "The Venturis I inspected were not fried by overheating. About half of the 496 valves that are installed are upside down. The exact count is being verified! I will be handed a big bill to fix the problem in the morning!"

The engineer responded, "Maybe you weren't listening when I told you it's impossible for the Venturis to be installed upside down by my machine!"

"Perhaps you should get on an airplane and see for yourself! I've got a showcase 496 valves-unit job full of problems!"

"I'm busy. You better figure it out yourself. The one thing I'll say…again…is that Venturis cannot be installed upside down by my machine! Period! You better get that through your hard head!"

I'll sum up the entire dilemma. The bill for the repairs was for $30,000. When Gunslinger handed it to me, I hoped desperately that my feet shaking in my loafers wasn't obvious. It was a huge labor bill! Easily the largest I had ever seen! I rationalized that given the size of the job, it might be okay…maybe! I stood motionless.

The handgun strapped to the Gunslinger's leg was prominently visible. I stared at the infamous bill and then at the scowl on Gunslinger's face. I thought about the field inspection I had done and the conversation with the engineer. Venturis danced in my head helter-skelter! The dollar amount of the request, right or wrong, was far beyond my level of authority. Nonetheless, I fired back boldly, with all the confidence I could muster up, "I'll take care of it!"

I knew I had stepped far onto the edge of a limb, but hoped, given the circumstance, my decision was justifiable!

The bold (stupid?) move led to a call from my guardian angel and boss, Roger Garrison, and Bill Ficken, his boss. Based on the engineering report, Bill was sure I had lost my mind.

Were it not for my solid track record with the company, and more importantly, Roger's vehement support of my decision, I surely would have been fired.

To soften the blow to the factory, I negotiated a program with my friend George Shoen, whose company supplied the job. Kelly's Pipe and Supply would credit the Gunslinger's account for the labor. Kelly's would accept no-charge product as compensation. By doing that, Moen's out of pocket expense was reduced 66%...which took some of the sting out of the bite.

Months later, I received a letter explaining that Moen's review of the issue confirmed that, amazingly, BOTH the engineer and I were correct. Yes, it was impossible for the machine to install the Venturis upside down! And yes, some valves were shipped with upside down Venturis. Explanation: To facilitate the rush on the order, the factory added a line that manually inserted the Venturis. The worker on the line was not trained to understand the critical nature of installing the Venturis a particular direction, so he installed them randomly; some right side up; some upside down. The unfortunate result was that the Gunslinger and I had an issue, causing both of us heartburn.

That explained just about everything except why the Gunslinger mysteriously disappeared after the completion of that project.

"A Reputable Rep is an extension of the manufacturer: conducting business with high ethics; caring about customers and solving their problems. They sell by relationship building...not just price."

— **Tom Schoendorf, Highland Tank**

Fundamentals of a Reputable Rep…

Scheduling regular meetings to discuss opportunities.

Working together as a team towards common goals.

Creating workable plans to buy, promote, and sell lines of products to the end-user.

Promptly follow-up!

Being punctual to appointments!

Knowing the market and how to serve it.

Training our people!

Creating pull-through business.

Understanding our business model. All wholesalers are not alike.

Building a partnership and relationship based on honesty and trust.

— Fred Laube, Director of Corporate Operations,
Hirsch Pipe and Supply

PART 8

THE SUM OF THE PARTS

Every rep, factory man, or distributor sales person has their own way of getting things done. We are all unique! My hope is that my stories, insights from industry leaders, and way of doing business will inspire people new to the business to make their own mark by exploring trails that are less traveled by their competitors. In keeping with plumbing industry humility, I'll leave you with this nugget from my friend Joe Maiale…

> "Henry, a well-known manufacturer's rep passed away. At the services someone asked, 'What did Henry have'? The reply was from a manufacturer's rep also attending the funeral, 'Well, to name a few, Bradford White, Sioux Chief, Sharkbite and Jacuzzi!'"
>
> **— Joe Maiale, VP Sales, InSinkErator**

LONG LIVE THE REPUTABLE REP!

ACKNOWLEDGMENTS

This book would not be possible without the help of my team of "BOOK BUDDIES" who inspire me, keep me straight, and roll up their sleeves when I need help. This teamwork ensures my books are the best they can be. My hope is that I've created a literary keepsake that readers enjoy and recommend to others.

Beverly Schmalhofer
Chief Editor who keeps me grounded

Patti Plummer and Joe Notte
MGA2

Carrie and Peggy @ Author's Marketing Experts
Marketing wizards that connect readers to my books

Mike and Linda Edmonds
Pre-readers and this author's biggest fans

Carmen and Eunice Catania
Pre-readers who inspire me to keep writing

Bruce Carnevale
Industry Consultant

Bob Russak
A Jelly Beans fan who guides me through legalities

Lisa Rogal
Facebook administrator

Bailey Rogal
Consultant

Dan Rogal
Website Designer

Andrea Douglas
Administrator

Al Cassidy
Artist-Created the book cover for Reputable Rep

Arron Sanders
Amazon connection

Debbie Perkins
Approvals and protections

CONTRIBUTOR INDEX

Bill Glockner, Hirsch Pipe & Supply

Bob Berumen, Hirsch Pipe & Supply

Bob Carnevale, Bradford White Corporation

Bob Riggs, Winnleson™

Bruce Carnevale, Bradford White Corporation

Chris Semerau, Reliance Worldwide Corporation

Dean Armstrong, Ferguson Enterprises, Inc.

Fred Laube, Hirsch Pipe & Supply

Gary Grosslight, Ferguson Enterprises, Inc.

Gregg Ferguson, Ferguson Enterprises, Inc.

Jeff Davis, Reliance Worldwide Corporation

Joe Maiale, InSinkErator

Joe Cicora, Red White Valve

John Potter, Ferguson Enterprises, Inc.

John Warner, Laars Heating Systems Co.

Kendrick Reaves, Reliance Worldwide Corporation

Kirk Livernash, Signature Sales, Inc.

Louie Armstrong, Ferguson Enterprises, Inc.

Mark Taylor, Bradford White Corporation

Michael Foster, Sioux Chief

Mike Lorber, Ferguson Enterprises, Inc.

Nick Giuffre, Bradford White Corporation

Mike Streator, Streator Pipe and Supply

Robert Garcia, Plumbing Wholesale Outlet

Ron Bradford, Signature Sales

Ron Kern, Ferguson Enterprises, Inc.

Russ Long, Ferguson Enterprises, Inc.

Steve Grosslight, Ferguson Enterprises, Inc.

Steve Shipley, Hirsch Pipe & Supply

Tod Minato, Firefighter Gas Safety Products

Tom Schoendorf, Highland Tank Manufacturing Company, Inc.

9 780998 132563